By Melanie Nunez

Table of Contents

Copyright	3
The Poems You'll @Your Valentine	5
About the book	7
Facebook	8
Twitter	14
Tumblr	17
Instagram	22
The Notes in Your iPhone	26
Thank You, for reading.- Melanie Nunez	30

Copyright

Author
Melanie Nunez

Editors
Rosalind Kingsley
Oswald Rojas

Cover Artist
Melanie Nunez

United States Copyright Office

Copyright © 2016

The Poems You'll @ Your Valentine

First Published using Papyrus, 2013

Kindle Direct Publishing

This book may be purchased for educational, business, or sales promotional use. Online edition is also available for this title. For more information, contact our institutional sales department:

inexcusablypoetic@gmail.com

While every precaution has been taken in the preparation of this book, the publisher and author assume no responsibility for errors or omissions, or for damages resulting from the use of the information contained herein.

The Poems You'll @ Your Valentine

By Melanie Nunez

About the book

In an age that is surrounded by social media we find ourselves dissolved from art and less impressed. This art however is about romanticizing the human being as a lover and friend. This is the art you can post to your feed and know it means something that only you two know. This is that book, that you @YourValentine on when you see a quote you know they'll recognize.

Ive read this book about 100 times and even though i'm not in love it makes me want to be and not even in a bad way. Read this book and you'll see what I mean there will be at least 1 poem that you will understand completely. It'll be that poem you'll post on Facebook, or Twitter, or instagram, or Tumblr, or maybe the one you copy into your phone's notes for when you need the feeling.

It's all about sharing the feeling now in days.

Facebook

Add Me First

I don't want to be the girl who plays hard to get but, add me first.

I want you to know what it feels like to wait I want you to stalk my page, which you have admitted to having found all on your own.

Add me.

I want you to make me have to change my relationship status to it's complicated. I want you to realize all the repetition in the poem,

I'm trying to make you see things indirectly.

Did you find my point?

Don't Poke Me

Did I hurt your feelings, I'm sorry I truly am but I just wanted to let you know that I'm your biggest fan. You are my starlight glimmer, and I'm just trying to keep you in here.

I'm just trying to make your time.

I'll stick around if that's fine, I can't guarantee I won't make you cry.

But we are together what you call an upside down tornado,

and you are looking so strong, so magnificent in this moment in time so don't move, forget about what we said you've been the only one in my head.

Change my Relationship Status

You think you are so cool, and you are.

But why do you have to be so cool about it.

This is how my mind feels about us, this is how my mind feels.

Jargon and a bunch of CD's I want to listen to while looking at nothing but your eyes.

Do you hear that?

Do you hear how loud my heart is beating.

Can you hear how strong it is?

Please don't forget to bring your CD's, my iTunes account doesn't work with my ghettoblaster.

Hey, you bring the ones that have lyrics we can think about can you bring some Tupac and Lauryn Hill 98'

We are the mark of our time, we are artists romanticizing the human condition. The pairs we make are worth romanticizing let the world know.

Switch your Facebook settings.

Little Secrets

Can I tell you a secret?

Your hands are sometimes cold enough to raise the hairs on my back, and when you touch me I have a mild heart attack.

I want you to familiarize yourself with the term falling?

because that's something i've been doing everyday it's you and I.

Baby, have you gotten this feeling too.

You have me looking at the sky wondering from which angle did you fall through.

So can you keep a secret, will you promise not to post it on Facebook,

I love you.

Letter to my Friends List

 Dear Friends, It's been awhile since we've spoken and I know I haven't posted much or posted up.

I know I haven't shown it much, but I love you.

Although each of you have a different story, we all know why each of us are important.

We used to ride to school together on the bus all of us, we'd swore we'd never grow up.

 Although we're older we're not as spirited as we were as kids.

Hard times and a lot of work and some of us have kids.

There is still all love.

Good job growing up.

You're Mine: A Sonnet

 I have an issue i'd like to share

 I took one look into your eyes and, I can't stop feeling like i'm falling. You touched my heart when your fingers touched my hair.

I'm not trying to be persistent but when are you calling,

Please don't play with my heart.

I'm not usually this persistent,

you tear me apart.

That's why i've been acting this distant,

But I need you more than you need me

I want to show you that I mean it

I want to show you how we could be

Just open your eyes a little wider to see it.

So i'll ask if i'll have you, ever.

You responded "baby, you'll have me forever"

Let your petals fall

If you were a rose you'd be so red, i'd mistake you for blood.

No, i'd mistake you for love.

With petals too strong to fall but, I just wanted to see if you love me or you love me not.

Your thorns haven't pricked me yet, so I guess it's safe to assume that you trust me.

It's okay to confess that you love me.

Titanic

I hear they're rebuilding the Titanic exactly how the first one looked.

If I ever step inside that ship, I want to be holding your hand.

I want to be held over the railing while my arms find home in the wind, I want to know you won't let go.

If we hit an iceberg, we can share the door.

You could hold my heart it'll keep you warm.

Wait

I hear you've been stalking my timeline, I hear you've combed through the years and examined every product.

I hear you've trespassed into my heart, I hear you know the ways, and where I hide the key.

Please don't steal, it'd mean alot to me.

Put out your hands,

You are fond of me, and of that I am so guilty.

Pleasure.

I want you to continue to find me in my poetry, but only when you miss me.

Check your timeline I tagged you in something.

You Know Who You Are

You know I promised not to be too soft, but you are the one person I don't mind reading poetry too when it's 2AM and I fall asleep on you. Or you on me, you're such a baby.

Will you be my baby?

I've been stalking your Facebook lately, I've been writing about you lately.
 This doesn't happen to often,
I'm the girl who never minded being alone until she was away from you.
I want to stay with you.

Twitter

140 Characters

Remember how I told you the sky is falling, I realized it was just the way I feel when you're holding my hand. Like falling. Don't you stop it.

Don't Ask Me

Kiss me, my lips want to tell you something. Don't ask me they are very secretive, Come here my eyes want to show you something. Don't ask me.

Confidently

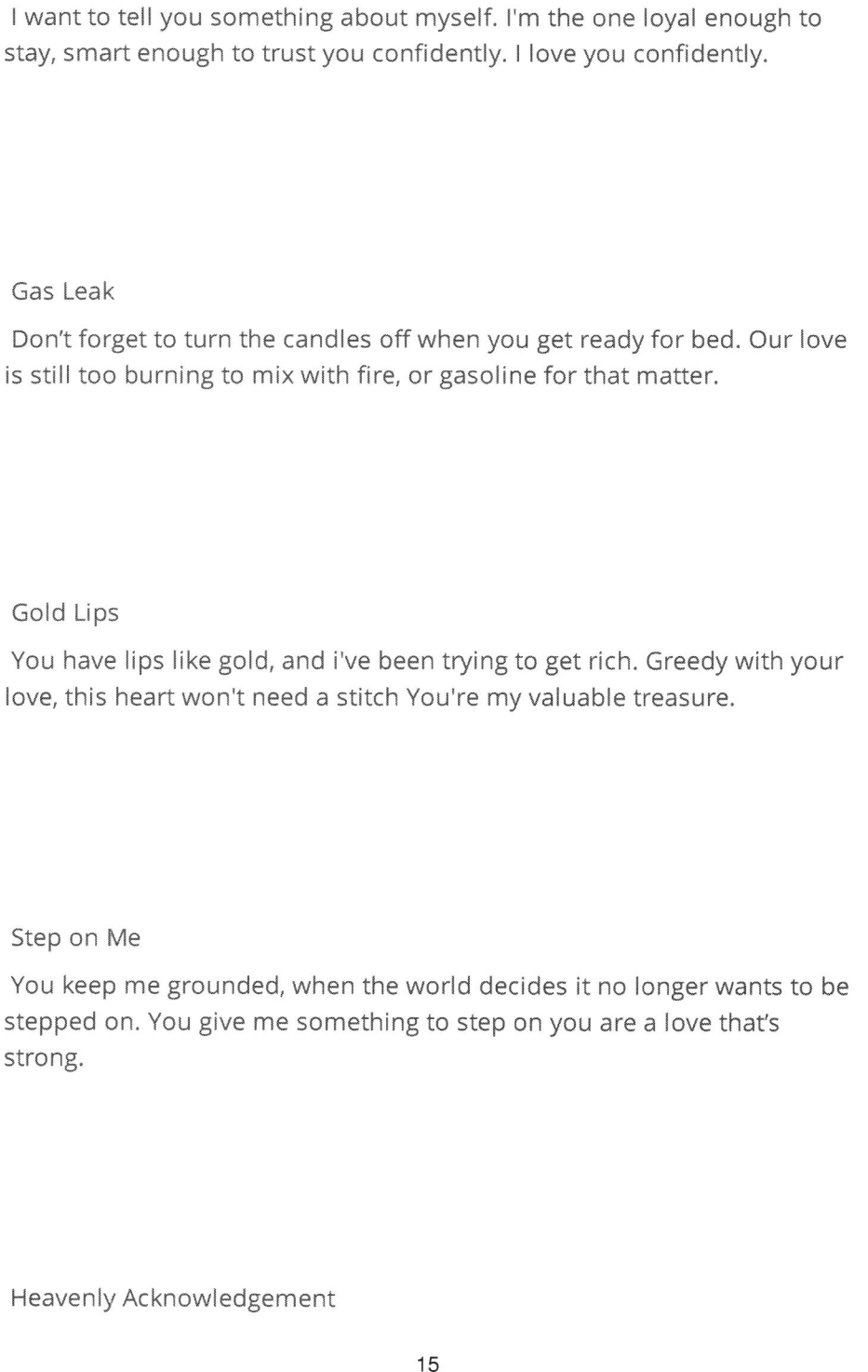

I want to tell you something about myself. I'm the one loyal enough to stay, smart enough to trust you confidently. I love you confidently.

Gas Leak

Don't forget to turn the candles off when you get ready for bed. Our love is still too burning to mix with fire, or gasoline for that matter.

Gold Lips

You have lips like gold, and i've been trying to get rich. Greedy with your love, this heart won't need a stitch You're my valuable treasure.

Step on Me

You keep me grounded, when the world decides it no longer wants to be stepped on. You give me something to step on you are a love that's strong.

Heavenly Acknowledgement

On this cloud we've been sitting on it's like we are higher than most in the game of love, Baby we are winning and even the angels above agree.

Love Doesn't Cost A Thing

I'll play my scratchers everyday, in hopes of winning someone like you, i'll throw all my money away if it meant I just got to talk to you.

Seeing in Colors

My red hands and your purple eyes, your yellow smile. You have a pink heart and blue hands. Hold my hand, I want to make purple with you.

If Twitter

Can I tell you how I feel in 140 words, and can you explain how this is real in just three words. You are the strength I use to get through the earthquake. Keep me stable. I want to express something to you, follow me. Make me think about why you haven't texted me back make me love sick. God knows I haven't been in so long. Make me want to dance on each one of these words make me want to make you the blessing to my curse. I need you now in less than 140 words.

Tumblr

Finding you in the Creases

I'm still trying to find the meaning behind these poems, I'm trying to see if they have to do with anything other than you.
You've flooded my pages darling.
And I've been drowning in a sea of thoughts you only seem to rescue me from.
Please don't be modest,
You are the most beautiful strength.
You make me catch my breath
So allow me to analyze my phrases
Allow me to find something more
You are the more.

Thinking about you

I've been looking at you a lot lately, thinking about you a lot lately.
I thought it'd just be after we get crazy.

But baby, I can't deny you been on my mind.
You have arms of royalty, I want to write on your body.
Your skin is killing me softly, I want to give you my art without tainting your portrait
I want to add my initials but you are not mine to own.

Home

Can I call you home?
Actually I haven't been asking much permission lately, but can I call you baby?
I want to call you maybe.
You are a mystery I want to uncover.
You are my favorite lover.
You.
Have not seemed to get off my mind.

I Still Remember

I wanted to write a poem you could keep to your heart, a poem that's words could understand your soul.
My love I know, I know that you are tired of all this hate it's gotten so obnoxious I agree.
My love I know, I know some nights it's hard to breath.
My love I know everything you do sometimes falls back onto your lap, but I know you're stronger than the relapse I know you could drop kick anyone who pisses you off.
That's why I love you.
You thought I didn't notice didn't you?
Loving you is like looking for green goats in India, loving you is never simple.
Loving you is a roller coaster with no breaks, I know when the falls are coming

so I'll prepare us for the next one, I've learned your eyes.
I've learned how easily you soak up pain.
You never let me take what isn't mine.
 Like you.
Yet, why is that I feel like I need you?
Why is that I feel like you need me.
Why is it that the only lips I miss are yours, pictures can't describe what touch remembers.
I remember.

You Know What to Do

 We were out of time and out of placement, why do I make finding my muse so complicated.
When we both know that my muse could be found in their walk or in the things they left behind, it is not that hard to find.
I think I find my muse when I fly, because I can't seem to not write about the sky from this cloud I'm sitting on.
 They sit on a throne of compassion never holding anything else then my passion never holding anything else than my uncertainty rotting underneath their skin.
 Waiting to be moist again.

Don't Forget to Smile

 When you wake up and they're already gone, and you remember their lips while you're showering to your favorite song.
 When the reminiscing lasts long and the memories keep collecting.
 When their kisses are worth collecting when their mind is worth remembering.

You'll come home to tangled bedsheets.
The kind that hold poetry behind the creases.
The kind that pleases.
The kind that's memory never seems to forget to smile.

Creative Juices

I remember that morning it rained, your lips puckered slow like poetry. Your nose crinkled and I swear before I said goodbye, your eyes, they said write about me.
Yet you never asked to be made a canvas out of.
You are the only art there is worth talking about these days.
Maybe it's too early and too cold or maybe I just don't like sleeping alone.
Maybe my pen thinks you are just as amazing as I do, maybe this paper agrees.
You've become my favorite muse right next to these flowers.
Maybe even more, you see that smile says write about me, your fingers combing through my hair say write about me, your mind says write about me, and I listen every time.
You don't know that I'm writing about you now, I have to let these creative juices out, before I drown.
Your head is resting on my chest.
Everything about this screams write about me.
But letting go of you is not an option.

I Can Make You Stay

You may have thought you left me, but I could tap into my memories whenever I want.
I could still recall the scent on your skin, the scent of our sins.

You can't leave, when I've already kept you prisoner in my mind.
You leave.
Memories stay.
I'll let the memories play, I'll reminisce all day.
When I begin to forget you, I'll buy your scent in the lovers isle at Walmart and start over.

We Woke Up Like This

Sometimes you feel guilty, and then there are the times you don't, the times you wish you would swallow down enough courage, to fill a bed of roses poetic enough for their head.
Or when they buy you flowers, or when they let you lay your head on their shoulder because all your poetry went black.
When they bring you back and say well look at that,
Can I take you home?
You don't know I'm writing this poem, They don't know their words hit home, They don't know.
They've been the subject to my words lately.
Subject: I'm falling.

Celebrity Crush

Are you familiar with the frustration of not being loved, but being in love. So so in love.
You've been drooling over love poems you know you'll never send.
So let's play pretend let's act like there is someone out there and I bet you there is.
I may be waiting, but I swear I found love in your lips.
Please keep speaking, can you spare me a kiss.

Instagram

Picture This

I've been on your Instagram staring at the same picture with the same smile and those same eyes and I just can't help but grin a little harder. Don't ask me why i'm smiling at my phone, and please don't peak.
I've been reading our conversations back to myself, is that weird?
I just want to picture your words in my head just so I could hear your voice again.

Captivated

Don't misinterpret the way that I look at you i've been thinking about you lately and only my thoughts know this inside joke.
You are so cute, when you're mad.
Allow me to tell you that you are a picture perfect version of royalty.
You are everything to me.
Please don't misinterpret my tired eyes for lack of love i've been captivated by you since I first saw you.

Big Eyes

I don't think it's appropriate for you to look at me like that, with your big grey eyes and your mouth saying words. You know the kind of words that stimulate my mind, that's why I love you. The all work no play you. The you should just stay, you. The don't play any games, you. I want you the same.

It Happens

I want to hold my breath, just long enough to inhale every inch of oxygen that has ever passed through your lips. I want to breath in enough, so that I don't choke when we kiss. You make my heart stop, while showing me that a heart should beat like this. Every beat has a pattern to unique not to understand.

A.A Meetings

You remind me of medical descriptions for illegal narcotics. Addictive, is usually the first word of each sentence. Just like your name lately, it's been the first word in each one of my thoughts. You've got me caught don't you? I've noticed because the A.A meetings make me want to text you, and ask if I could see you awhile. I have 4 patches on but I still want you. I'm addicted, to you.

Too Much Art in You

I think I should apologize, i've made a canvas out of you. This ink has taken advantage of you too, using my thoughts of you as art for this page, so please excuse this page. I've made a canvas of your name, Please don't be ashamed, I usually make a canvas of my pain, But you are not that kind of art. You are the shakespearean influence, causing me to compare you to a summer's day. We'll make roses grow from concrete if it's okay.

Shh Don't Tell

Please don't tell anyone i'm soft, because when you smile I hope you know you make my heart beat a little faster. Please don't tell anyone that you and a little laughter, equals a nomination to my favorite disaster. That I can't seem to stop writing about. Listen. I know this is a lot to chew, but I think my pen is in love with you.

Fall asleep on me

Don't tell anyone I read you my poetry at 2AM when the boogie man has started tossing and turning under your bed, and there is just too much thunder clouding your head. Don't you tell anybody, that i'm ten poems into tonight and they're all about you. Don't tell anybody i've been thinking about you. I'm already thinking about the next one, which will probably end up being about you. All these poems want to do, is talk about you.

Why Forget

You screenshot my lock screen, and said remember this. However, I just remember your lips asking me for a kiss. You are my bliss, serenity at it's finest. You are always at your finest, don't be embarrassed I like it. So don't be anything else, who am I kidding you're too 100 for that.

Walk with me

I just want to see you for this one last time, I just want to be with you for this one last time. I want to take your time. I want to stop saying these rhymes every time I see you. You're so hardcore, and I like that. I like you, and that's what scares me. This is scary, will you be my baby? will you walk with me for the rest of my life, or can you just walk with me?

The Notes in Your iPhone

Smile

Don't close your eyes I want to see your pupils dilate when I get closer. Hold my hand, I want to make your hands warmer. I can't keep confessing things to you, without out saying them out loud. Your heart beats so loud, Let's log out of this social media haze, lets write poems to each other that we'll keep in our phones for a rainy day. When we can't stop smiling at each other, just keep on smiling at me lover. We were made for one another.

O2

You flow right through me. I never felt more out of breath, then the time that you were not around. You've been on my mind, and i'd advise you check the time because we've been lost in conversation for 2 hours. I can't stop wondering where the time went, I still feel like the first day I saw you, every time I see you. You are unbelievable. You keep me guessing, and that's just what I need.

Trade

Have I gone too far? Please tell me now if I have, because I am not too sure which one of your hearts to grab. Yours or mine, but you use them both so we'll that I can't make up my mind Am I out of time? how about I keep your heart, and you could keep mine. Make sure to wear it on your sleeve, I want people to see.

FaceTime

I must have been asleep when you called me, because darling I've been waiting to hear your voice all day trust me, I was waiting for you to call me. I love it when you're calling. FaceTime me. I want to see that laugh in person, I want to see you talk with such passion I want to watch you talk. You are so intriguing, I just can't get enough of you. Don't tell anyone.

Are We More Than Friends ?: A Sonnet

I like the way you smell, when you hold me in so closely.
I don't think you should tell,
but I've been writing about you mostly.
I know some things are better left untouched,
Yet sometimes this is torture.
I'm not asking for much,
just tell me this is for sure.
So when you say I'm yours,
I will profess that you are mine.
I'll give you the keys to all my doors,
and all of my free time.
It has to be your eyes so blue,
because I am just so infatuated with you.

Well Hello

What's the matter with you? I was just perfectly fine being alone, until you came along making me feel these constant butterflies. Who sent you? Was it cupid? Oh that son of a bitch did it again. He loves to play with my head. You love to play with my head, don't you? I just keep falling for you. I wasn't ready, and here you are. Next time I'll probably still wish on that shooting star.

You Know This

Let me tell you something important, let me tell you something from my heart; let me tell you something. I've been with you for a while now and I just want to say that you are so special to me. For example, when I go grocery shopping I always see the things you'd like to try. I've been putting you first and I can't seem to figure out why. Baby, I am way more yours than you are mine.

Make Me Jealous

You know you made me jealous. You know I like you too much to say that out loud. You know I'm softer than this façade, and this facade has always been the best actor. But what is your act for? Because I think I've gotten you figured out. I think you have hands that been through some hits, but can still hold me softer than the way you blink your eyes. I'm hypnotized by those eyes. That look that tells me everything, just so that I don't look inside.

Bad Love

I'm not yet a villain to myself, but when I am i'll let you take my hand and make things sweet again.
I want you to make things sweet again.
I haven't had much of you lately but I've sure been missing you.
You know us girls always want what they say is bad for you.

But darling, you are so right and so so sweet, and I need you to take this dark and turn it white.
I love you. Please call soon, Your Valentine.

I Won't Tell A Soul

You held me like I was going to leave you, you didn't let go.
I prayed you wouldn't let go, and you didn't not even when your breathing got heavy, and your muscles loosened.
You held me to your chest.
Your heart told me the rest.
I promise I won't repeat what I hear.

Thank You, for reading.

- Melanie Nunez

Made in the USA
Columbia, SC
26 October 2023